12 more CLASSIC JAZZ STANDARDS
with Two All-Star Rhythm Sections

T0085260

PLAYBACK+
Speed • Pitch • Balance • Loop

To access audio visit:
www.halleonard.com/mylibrary

Enter Code
6953-7845-2575-0672

ISBN 978-1-59615-690-6

Music Minus One

EXCLUSIVELY DISTRIBUTED BY

HAL•LEONARD®

Visit Hal Leonard Online at
www.halleonard.com

Contact us:
Hal Leonard
7777 West Bluemound Road
Milwaukee, WI 53213
Email: info@halleonard.com

In Europe, contact:
Hal Leonard Europe Limited
42 Wigmore Street
Marylebone, London, W1U 2RN
Email: info@halleonardeurope.com

In Australia, contact:
Hal Leonard Australia Pty. Ltd.
4 Lentara Court
Cheltenham, Victoria, 3192 Australia
Email: info@halleonard.com.au

TWELVE MORE CLASSIC JAZZ STANDARDS

In the year 1955, I assembled three rhythm sections to record twenty-four songs, each performing eight of them. I distinctly remember calling them for these sessions, and the enormous relief I felt as each accepted the gig. I knew I was hiring the best in the land. These men, the cream of the crop as their brief biographies below will attest, and their efforts, recorded on Sunday afternoons at Steinway Hall, became the basis for the MMO library's early success. These performances sold tens of thousands of albums and were the backbone for underwriting the later expansion of the MMO catalogue. Their efforts came to be known around the world as the very best rhythm section tracks one could acquire to perform jazz standards. To have these players together on sessions was a dream-come-true for me, as the producer, a drummer, and an avid follower of their careers in music. It's sixty years later and these sessions are indelibly fixed in my minds-eye and memory. One example; Pettiford was assigned a bass solo on *Poor Butterfly* and was working out the routine, when Kenny Clarke said, *'come on man, it's only jazz'* , well Pettiford's glance alone spoke volumes and Clarke fell into immediate silence, Oscar was not someone to mess with! The solo by the way is worth the price of admission. I always think of it as a guitar solo played on the bass. It was so gentle, graceful and all-of-one piece.

Don Abney, *Pianist,* (March 10, 1923 - Jan. 20, 2000) Studied at Manhattan School of Music. Returning from service in the middle 40s he played with Kai Winding, Wilbur de Paris, Bill Harris, Chuck Wayne, Sy Oliver and Louis Bellson. He recorded with Armstrong, Benny Carter, Oscar Pettiford, Carmen McRae, Sarah, Eartha Kitt, and Pearl Bailey. Don moved to Hollywood, and worked as a musical director at Universal and MCA, and appeared as the pianist in "Peter Kelly's Blues" behind Ella Fitzgerald. Abney toured with Anita O'Day in the 80's. In the 90's he moved to Japan and toured for several years with considerable success. He returned to the USA where he passed in January of 2000. We were fortunate to have him on our original three rhythm section albums in 1953.

Jimmy Raney, *Guitar,* (1927 - May 10, 1995) Born in Louisville, Kentucky, was most notable for his work from 1951 – 1952 and 1962-1963 with Stan Getz and for his work from 1953 to 1954 with the Red Norvo trio, replacing Tal Farlow. In 1954 and 1955 he won the Downbeat critics poll for guitar. His first paying gig was in Chicago with the Max Miller Quartet at Elmer's in Chicago. Raney also worked with the Artie Shaw Orchestra and collaborated with Woody Herman for a large part of 1948. He also collaborated and recorded with Buddy DeFranco, Al Haig and Bob Brookmeyer. In 1967, personal and professional difficulties led him to leave NY and return to Louisville. He resurfaced in the 1970s and did work with his son Doug, also a guitarist. Raney suffered from Mèniére's disease, a degenerative disease that led to almost complete deafness in both ears, although this did not stop him from playing. He died of heart failure in Louisville on May 10,1995, just short of his 68th birthday. His obituary in the New York Times called him "one of the most gifted and influential postwar jazz guitarists in the world".

Oscar Pettiford, *Bassist,* (Sept. 30, 1922 - Sept. 8, 1960) Pettiford was born in Okmulgee, Okla. His mother was Choctaw and his father was half Cherokee and half African American. He grew up playing in the family band in which he sang and danced before switching to piano at the age of 12, then to double bass when he was 14. He is quoted as saying he did not like the way people were playing the bass so he developed his own way of playing it. Despite being admired by the likes of Milt Hinton at the age of 14, he gave it up in 1941 as he did not believe he could make a living. Five months later, he once again met Hinton, who persuaded him to return to music. In 1942 he joined the Chas. Barnett band and in 1943 gained wider public attention after recording with Coleman Hawkins on his "The Man I Love". Pettiford also recorded with Earl Hines and Ben Webster around this time. He and Dizzy Gillespie led a bop group in 1943. In 1945 Pettiford went with Hawkins to California, where he appeared in Crimson Canary, a mystery movie known for its jazz soundtrack. He then worked with Duke Ellington from 1945 to 1948 and for Woody Hermann 1949 before working mainly as a leader in the 1950s. Pettiford also introduced the cello to the world of jazz, become a proficient soloist on the instrument. It became his secondary instrument throughout the remainder of his career. He died in Copenhagen, Denmark. He recorded extensively during the 1950s for Debut, Bethlehem and ABC Paramount labels and for European companies after he moved to Copenhagen in 1958. Along with his contemporary, Chas.Mingus, Pettiford stands out as one of the most recorded bass-playing band leaders/composers in jazz.

Kenny Clarke, *Drummer,* performed in Pittsburgh as a teenager. He later joined Roy Eldridge, playing with the bands of Lonnie Simmons, Edgar Hayes, Claude Hopkins, and Teddy Hill in 1939-40 where a co-member was Dizzy Gillespie. Thelonious Monk, Charlie Christian and Bud Powell began an extraordinary series of jam sessions leading to the development of be bop. He developed the practice of interjecting off-beat accents on snare and bass drum against a steady pulse. After Army service in 1943- 46 he returned to the States and recorded with Tadd Dameron, Dizzy and Fats Navarro. In 1951 he joined the Milt Jackson Quartet, the forerunner of the Modern Jazz Quartet, performing until 1955. In '56 he moved to Paris to work with Bud Powell's Trio (1959-62). From 1960 to 1973 with Francy Boland in France he led the Clarke-Boland Octet and Big Band. Kenny also appeared in several French films and although making occasional concert tours in the USA, Clarke continued to perform, record and teach in Europe until his death in 1985.

Clarke enjoyed a reputation as one of the most sensitive and innovative jazz musicians. With Gillespie he revolutionized the drummer's technique by shifting the steady 4/4 pulse from the bass drum to the ride cymbal, thereby allowing the use of the bass and snare drum for independent counter-rhythms in support of the improvising musicians. Among Clarke's compositions are the well-known Salt Peanuts (written with Gillespie) and Epistrophy (with Monk)

Mundell Lowe, *Guitar,* Born in Laurel, Miss. on April 21, 1922 - In the '30s he played country music and Dixieland jazz. He later played with big bands and on television in New York City. In the 1960s, Lowe composed music for films and television in both NY and Los Angeles. He performed and/or recorded with Billie Holiday, Bobby Darin, Lester Young, Charlie Parker, Bill Evans, Helen Humes, Roy Buchanan, Charles Mingus, Stan Getz, Doc Severinsen, Kai Winding, Sarah Vaughan, Carmen McRae, Benny Carter, Herb Ellis, Tal Farlow, Barry Manilow, Andre Previn, Ray Brown, Kiri Te Kanawa, Tete Montoliu, Harry Belafonte and hosts of other famed performers. Lowe was responsible for introducing pianist Bill Evans to producer Orrin Keepnews resulting in Evan's first recordings under his own leadership.

During the late 1970s and early '80s Lowe was also a well-respected teacher at Dick Grove Music Workshop, later the Grove School of Music in Studio City, Ca., one of the top professional level music schools in the world. He taught guitar as well as scoring. In 1998, Mundell was inducted into the Mississippi Music Hall of Fame,and in 1999 Millsaps College in Jackson conferred an honorary Doctorate of Arts on Mr. Lowe in recognition of his lifetime of outstanding musical accomplishments. On July 17, 2009 Mundell Lowe returned home to Laurel, the city he ran away from in 1938. In recognition of a lifetime of musical achievement he was given a key to the city and honored by the Mayor who proclaimed July 18, 2009 Mundell Lowe Day in Laurel.

Wilber Ware, *Bassist,* (Sept. 8, 1922 - Sept. 9, 1979) Born in Chicago, Ware taught himself to play banjo and bass and he approached the double bass not only as a melodic and rhythmic instrument but also a percussive instrument. In the 1940s, he worked with Stuff Smith, Sonny Stitt and Roy Eldridge. He recorded with Sun Ra in the early '50s. Later he settled in New York, and worked for MMO on the classic Jim Chapin album, Coordinated Independence. It was his first recording session in NY and the result of an article praising his work in Downbeat. I sought him out on arrival in the 'Big Apple' and engaged him for what became an iconic album in the MMO library, early in its foundation. Ware became a staff bassist for Riverside Records playing on many of the label's sessions with such diverse stylists as J.R.Monterose, Toots Thielemans, Tina Brooks, Zoot Sims and Grant Green.

Ware also performed with Eddie Vinson, Art Blakey and Buddy DeFranco. He's best known for his work with the Thelonious Monk quartet in 1957-58 and for his live recordings with Sonny Rollins Trio at the Village Vanguard. The best illustration of this is Ware's inter-play with Monk, in "Off Minor" (Take 5) as Monk and Ware create a piano-bass dialogue that increasingly builds a tension that is at last resolved with Ware's highly creative and angular extended bass solo that remains one of the finest ever recorded in modern jazz. Ware's unique ability to interpret Monk compositions, combined with his impeccable and swinging sense of time and his percussive attack, perhaps make Ware the most perfectly suited bassist to ever work with Monk. Sadly, Ware struggled with narcotics addiction that resulted in his return to Chicago in 1963 and a period when he was largely inactive for about six years. In 1969 he played with Clifford Jordan, Elvin Jones and Sonny Rollins. He later moved to Philadelphia where he died from emphysema in 1979.

Bobby Donaldson, *Drummer,* (Nov .29, 1922 - Boston 1971) After playing locally in the early 1940s, Donaldson played with Russell Rocoies while in service with the Army in NY City. In 1946-47 Donaldson worked with Cat Anderson, and following this played with Edmond Hall, Andy Kirk, Lucky Millinder, Buck Clayton, Red Norvo, Sy Oliver and Louis Armstrong. He was a prolific session musician for much of the 1950s and 1960s, playing with Helen Merrill, Ruby Braff, Mel Powell, Benny Goodman, Count Basie, Bobby Jaspar, Herbie Mann, Andrew Hodeir, Kenny Burrell, Lonnie Johnson, Frank Wess, Willie Jackson and Johnny Hodges. Bobby performed on many MMO albums at its inception in the early '50s. His playing was impeccable, rhythmic yet smooth, and perfectly formed for accompanying young players. He was a perfect foil for Geo. Duvivier's bass.

b INSTRUMENT

I May Be Wrong

Words and Music by HARRY RUSKIN and HENRY SULLIVAN

Too Marvelous For Words

Bb INSTRUMENT

Words & music by
Johnny Mercer
and Richard A. Whiting

4 choruses: 1st. You, 2nd. guitar solo 1st 16 bars
3rd. You, 4th. bass solo at bridge

Pg. 5

I Cover The Waterfront

Words by Edward Heyman
Music by Johnny Green

me.

Note:
bass solo 1st 8 bars
of the repeat.

Pg. 6

Fine And Dandy

Bb INSTRUMENT

Words and music by
Kay Swift & Paul James

Gee, it's all FINE AND DAN - DY,

Sug - ar Can - dy, When I've got you.

Then I on - ly see the sun - ny side,

E - ven troub - le has its fun - ny side.

When you're gone Sug - ar Can - dy,

I get lone - some I get so blue.

When you're han - dy it's FINE AND DAN - DY, But

when you're gone what can I do?

4 choruses:
3rd. split fours w/drums, (you start)

Pg. 7

Jeepers Creepers

Bb INSTRUMENT

Words and music by
Harry Warren & Johnny Mercer

5 choruses:
3rd. split fours w/piano (piano start)

My Heart Stood Still

Words and music by
George A. Rochberg

Bb INSTRUMENT

Piano solo 1st 8 bars of 2nd chorus.

Pg. 9

You Go To My Head

Words and music by
J. Fred Coots and
Haven Gillespie

Bb INSTRUMENT

Just One Of Those Things

Words and music by
Cole Porter

Bb INSTRUMENT

3 choruses:
2nd. Guitar solo to bridge.

Pg. 11

Crazy Rhythm

Bb INSTRUMENT

Words by Irving Caesar
Music by Joseph Meyer &
Roger Wolfe Kahn

6 choruses:
1st. Afro-Cuban except bridge.
2nd. You
3rd. Bass Solo
4th. Guitar Solo
5th. Piano Solo
6th. Afro-Cuban, Drum Solo on bridge.

Pg. 12

When Your Lover Has Gone

Words and music by
E.A. Swan

Don't Take Your Love From Me

Bb INSTRUMENT

Words and music by
Henry Nemo

2nd. chorus double time.

Bb INSTRUMENT

Strike Up The Band

Words by Ira Gershwin
Music by George Gershwin

5 choruses:
3rd. guitar solo
4th. split fours w/drums, (drums start)
5th. split fours w/bass 1st 16 bars (you start)

Pg. 15

I May Be Wrong

Eb INSTRUMENT

Words and Music by HARRY RUSKIN and HENRY SULLIVAN

Too Marvelous For Words

Eb INSTRUMENT

Words & music by
Johnny Mercer
and Richard A. Whiting

4 choruses: 1st. You,   2nd. guitar solo 1st 16 bars
3rd. You,   4th. bass solo at bridge

I Cover The Waterfront

Words by Edward Heyman
Music by Johnny Green

Eb INSTRUMENT

Note:
bass solo 1st 8 bars
of the repeat.

Fine And Dandy

Eb INSTRUMENT

Words and music by
Kay Swift & Paul James

4 choruses:
3rd. split fours w/drums, (you start)

Jeepers Creepers

Eb INSTRUMENT

Words and music by
Harry Warren & Johnny Mercer

5 choruses:
3rd. split fours w/piano (piano start)

Pg. 20

My Heart Stood Still

Words by LORENZ HART
Music by RICHARD RODGERS

Piano solo 1st 8 bars of 2nd chorus.

Pg. 21

You Go To My Head

Words and music by
J. Fred Coots and
Haven Gillespie

Eb INSTRUMENT

Pg. 22

6 choruses:
1st. Afro-Cuban except bridge.
2nd. You
3rd. Bass Solo
4th. Guitar Solo
5th. Piano Solo
6th. Afro-Cuban, Drum Solo on bridge. **Pg. 24**

When Your Lover Has Gone

Words and music by
E.A. Swan

Don't Take Your Love From Me

Words and music by
Henry Nemo

Strike Up The Band

Words by Ira Gershwin
Music by George Gershwin

Eb INSTRUMENT

Let the drums roll out!_____ Let the

Trum - pet call!_____ While the peo - ple shout!_____ STRIKE UP THE

BAND!_____ Hear the cym - bals ring!_____ Call - ing

one and all_____ To the mar - tial swing,_____ Strike up the

band!_____ There is work to be done, to be done! There's a

war to be won, To be won! Come, you son of a gun, Of a gun! Take your

stand!_____ Fall in line, you bo!_____ Come a -

long, let's go!_____ Hey, lead - er! STRIKE UP THE BAND!_____

5 choruses:
3rd. guitar solo
4th. split fours w/drums, (drums start)
5th. split fours w/bass 1st 16 bars (you start)

Pg. 27

I May Be Wrong

Too Marvelous For Words

BASS CLEF

Words & music by
Johnny Mercer
and Richard A. Whiting

You're just too mar - vel- ous, TOO MAR - VEL - OUS FOR WORDS, Like glo - ri - ous glam - or- ous and that old stand - by am - or- ous. It's all to won - der-ful, I'll nev - er find the words, That say e- nough, tell e- nough, I mean they just are'nt swell e- nough. You're much too much, and just too ver - y ver - y! To ev - er be in Web- ster's Dic- tion- a - ry, and so I'm bor - row-ing a love song from the birds, To tell you that you're mar - vel- ous, TOO MAR- VEL- OUS FOR WORDS. You're

4 choruses: 1st. You,   2nd. guitar solo 1st 16 bars
3rd. You,   4th. bass solo at bridge

I Cover The Waterfront

Words by Edward Heyman
Music by Johnny Green

BASS CLEF

Note:
bass solo 1st 8 bars
of the repeat.

Pg. 30

Fine And Dandy

Words and music by
Kay Swift & Paul James

Jeepers Creepers

BASS CLEF

Words and music by
Harry Warren & Johnny Mercer

5 choruses:
3rd. split fours w/piano (piano start)

Pg. 32

My Heart Stood Still

Words and music by
George A. Rochberg

Piano solo 1st 8 bars of 2nd chorus.

You Go To My Head

Words and music by
J. Fred Coots and
Haven Gillespie

BASS CLEF

Just One Of Those Things

Words and music by
Cole Porter

BASS CLEF

3 choruses:
2nd. Guitar solo to bridge.

Pg. 35

Crazy Rhythm

Words by Irving Caesar
Music by Joseph Meyer &
Roger Wolfe Kahn

BASS CLEF

6 choruses:
1st. Afro-Cuban except bridge.
2nd. You
3rd. Bass Solo
4th. Guitar Solo
5th. Piano Solo
6th. Afro-Cuban, Drum Solo on bridge.   **Pg. 36**

When Your Lover Has Gone

BASS CLEF

Words and music by
E.A. Swan

Pg. 37

Don't Take Your Love From Me

Words and music by
Henry Nemo

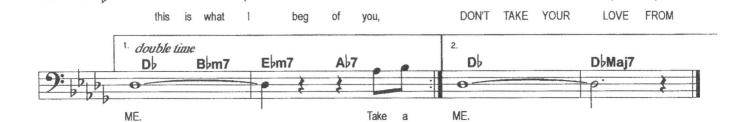

Strike Up The Band

Words by Ira Gershwin
Music by George Gershwin

BASS CLEF

5 choruses:
3rd. guitar solo
4th. split fours w/drums, (drums start)
5th. split fours w/bass 1st 16 bars (you start)

Pg. 39